KU-708-929

ANIMALS
AND THEIR YOUNG

PRINTED IN **DEAN &** **SON Ltd.** GREAT BRITAIN
52/54 Southwark St. LONDON SE1 1UA
TRADE MARK

© 1977 Dean & Son Ltd

3 08502 4

The African elephant is the largest of all land mammals. Both male and female have long ivory tusks and they live in well-organised herds, eating leaves, grasses and fruits.

Zebras live in large herds on the grassy plains of Africa. The female zebra has only one foal at a time.

Giraffes are the tallest animals in the world. They live in Africa and eat leaves and branches from the taller trees which only they can reach.

Newly-born lion cubs are spotted, but these markings fade in about six months. The parents and their young live together in family groups called prides.

Swans are the largest water birds. They build their nests on the edges of a river or lake, and both parents help to feed and guard the young swans, called cygnets.

The foal is born with its eyes open, and it can
soon run around the fields, although its long
legs are rather wobbly.

Seal pups are born with pale fur which soon turns darker. They can swim easily at an early age.

These lambs will grow up to provide us with warm wool to make our clothes and blankets.

Young koalas live in their mother's pouch until they are about two months old, then they are carried on her back. Koalas eat only eucalyptus leaves.

The red kangaroo of Australia can grow to a height of six feet and hop as far as twenty feet. It feeds on grass and leaves, and the female carries the young in her pouch for four months after birth.

Chimpanzees feed on fruits, leaves and nuts
in the wild. When in captivity they soon
learn to eat almost the same foods as man.
They are very intelligent, and can walk on
two legs.

The wild boar is the ancestor of our domestic pig. The females give birth to their litters in nests of branches on the ground.

Llamas live in South America. They are used as pack animals, and as a source of milk, wool and meat.

Badgers sleep in underground burrows, called sets, during the day and at night they come out to feed on insects and other small animals.

Young rabbits are born helpless, naked and blind. But soon they are able to run around in the fields, careful not to stray too far from mother.

The dromedary camel lives in Arabia and Egypt. It is used as a pack animal and can travel up to thirty miles a day. It is called the ship of the desert.

The white rhinoceros is really light grey in colour. It lives in Africa. A young rhinoceros stays with its parents until it is about half grown.

Harvest mice build their nests on stalks of wheat or corn. But when harvest comes, it's time to move.

The red squirrel is rare in Britain, but it is found all over Europe. It builds a round nest, called a drey, in a tree, and may have four babies in a litter.

A fallow deer and her calf. They eat grass and leaves and are found all over Europe and Asia Minor.

Tapirs live in swampy areas, and eat leaves and branches which they pull off with their flexible snouts. The young tapir will eventually lose its spots and stripes.

With their streamlined bodies and webbed feet, otters are well-adapted for life in the water. They feed on small fish, birds, insects and frogs.

Polar bears live in the northern polar regions and eat fish and seals. They have hair on the soles of their paws to give them a good grip on the ice. Eskimos hunt them for food and clothing.

Foxes are members of the dog family. They hunt at night and feed on small mammals, birds, insects and fruit.